GRE ... NERS

of ... lor

GREAT ATLANTIC LINERS

of the Twentieth Century in Color

WILLIAM H. MILLER & ANTON LOGVINENKO

AMBERLEY PUBLISHING

Cover Photo: White Star's *Olympic.*

Page 2 Photo: George Washington seen in the Boston Naval Shipyard.

Introduction Photo: Another White Star liner, the *Celtic,* is seen arriving in Boston harbor following a westbound crossing from Liverpool and Cobh.

Rear Cover Above: Bremen, one of Germany's most prestigious ships, at Bremerhaven.

Rear Cover Below: White Star's *Majestic* at New York.

First published 2013

Amberley Publishing Plc
The Hill, Stroud
Gloucestershire, GL5 4EP

www.amberley-books.com

Copyright © William H. Miller & Anton Logvinenko 2012

The right of William H. Miller & Anton Logvinenko
to be identified as the Authors of
this work has been asserted in accordance with the Copyrights,
Designs and Patents Act 1988.

ISBN 978 1 4456 0373 5

British Library Cataloguing in Publication Data.
A catalogue record for this book is available from the British Library.

Typeset in 10pt on 13pt Celeste.
Typesetting by Amberley Publishing.
Printed in the UK.

For all the great ocean liner collectors
who have gathered, saved and cherished the varied artifacts of the liners of the past:
they are preserving maritime history.

ACKNOWLEDGMENTS

Many other hands are involved in creating a book and together we extend our great appreciation. First and foremost, our thanks to Amberley Publishing, and especially to Campbell McCutcheon and Louis Archard for creating the final product. They do a superb job – and also in preserving ocean liner history.

And added special thanks to Allen Pellymounter for the initial introduction between the two co-authors.

Kind, generous and often patient collector-friends have assisted as well: Ernest Arroyo, Philippe Brebant, Richard Faber, Luis Miguel Correia, the late Alex Duncan, Andy Hernandez, Hisashi Noma and Albert Wilhelmi. Companies and organizations that have further assisted include: Cunard Line, French Line, Hapag-Lloyd, Moran Towing & Transportation Company, the Port Authority of New York & New Jersey, Steamship Historical Society of America and the World Ship Society.

FOREWORD

Forget everything. Forget everything you thought you knew up to this point.

I say these words every time someone asks me about picturing events that occurred many years ago. If you want to understand the people who lived in the early twentieth century, their motives and way of life, then you must forget the modern world and look at history through the eyes of people who lived at that time. And if I spoke about the imagination earlier, right now I say this in the most literal sense. Forget everything and look at the beginning of the twentieth century through the eyes of its contemporaries - look at the Great Atlantic Liners in color!

My name is Anton Logvinenko, and I was born in 1985, exactly fifteen days after Robert Ballard found the remains of the world's most famous ocean liner – the *Titanic*. My childhood dream was to be a sailor, an officer on a passenger steamer, but I studied law and eventually went to work in aviation. Nevertheless, my heart has always belonged to the sea and those classic liners that traversed the Atlantic.

It all started back in 1995 when I first read Walter Lord's *A Night to Remember*. This story fully captivated me as it did so many of us, and then came James Cameron's film and the subsequent 'titanicmania'. And my passion for the ship *Titanic* grew into a fascination with all the classic ocean liners of the early twentieth century.

Joining 'The Ship-Legend Titanic', the Russian Internet's largest forum dedicated to Olympic-class ships, was my initial entry into colorization. It was the first place where I had ever seen colorized photographs. While they were unsightly and coarse, with incorrect coloring and some details left totally uncolored, at the time it was a revelation. Even with their many imperfections, I thought I could never do something like that. Then I went into the army, and when I returned home I saw that this art had failed to advance. For example, colorists continued to paint the water at shipyards azure, as in the Caribbean or a resort pool. But of course the water is never this color at ports, instead taking on a muddy, swampy shade. So I decided to try colorizing a photo myself, simply in order to show what colors should be used. I had always wanted to do my small part to restore classic ocean liners to their former greatness and beauty. And so it became my hobby.

I am self-taught. I was never trained in Photoshop and did everything by trial and error. Looking back, I see that my initial works were far from perfect, so I have redone them. Did I pick the colors at random? No. I start work on each new photo by studying its history. The colors have been selected on the basis of intensive research. That is why the photographs you will see of your favorite liners look as if they were taken just yesterday. These are not drawings or computer models, just real colorized photographs.

I was occasionally asked to publish a book of my colorized photographs, but I had no idea how to do it. One day, Allen R. Pellymounter from southern California found my work on Facebook. He suggested that I contact his friend William Miller, and offer Mr Miller my colorized photos as illustrations for his book. And that's how it happened. This book was created due to Messrs Pellymounter and Miller. And for that I am extremely grateful!

At some point colorizing old photographs ceased to be simply my hobby and became my way of reviving the Great Atlantic liners, their beauty and grandeur. Of course, I am far from Ken Marschall, but this is my way of leaving something behind to the world.

So I invite you on a fascinating journey through time, back to the beginning of the twentieth century. You will not regret it!

Anton Logvinenko
Kiev, Ukraine
Summer 2012

INTRODUCTION

After more than eighty books, over a thousand articles and countless lectures aboard contemporary passenger ships, I seem to be propelled by own version of 'steam power' – there can never be enough documentation, record, mention of the great ocean liners. Once, we only had books, filled with words of history and numbers of specification, and of course some photos. Mostly, the pictures were in black and white, sometimes very detailed and possibly even dramatic views. These brought the ships to life. There are of course that army of fine marine artists, who have re-created – with the skill of hand and movement of brush – the liners in varied moods: sailing across sun-drenched waters, in turbulent seas, in tropic settings, in misty fog, aglow in nighttime. Then, more recently, came the age of video film – seeing the liners in even greater glory: sailing, arriving, steaming, smoking, even sinking. And of course there are the all but mind-boggling recreations of the great liners such as the immortal *Titanic* in James Cameron's $1 billion, blockbuster film of 1997 and then, in even bigger-than-life form, in the 3D version introduced in 2012. It has all been magic, a wealth of material and background – and inspiration and sheer pleasure.

In this book, we have something of a unique touch – colorized photos of some of the greatest liners of the twentieth century. Through Anton Logvinenko's very interesting, clever, detailed efforts, these 'floating palaces' come to life again. The colors and so the detail are superb – myself, I can all but see the splendor of the four-funnel *Mauretania* at New York, the *Lusitania* at the City's brand new Chelsea Piers, those German four-stackers and the might and proportions of the likes of the *Imperator* and *Vaterland*, and even the curious 'dazzle paint' configurations aboard the likes of the wartime *Olympic*. Of course, the endlessly appealing *Titanic* receives significant attention.

Fine actual color photography was well in place by the 1950s and 60s and so Anton and I decided to conclude our list with the likes of the *Rotterdam*, *France* and *Leonardo da Vinci*. They were in fact the final generation of Atlantic liners for such cross-ocean stalwarts as the Holland-America, French and Italian lines. Coincidentally, the 1960s was the age in which the Atlantic liner was in fact drawing to a dramatic, all but sudden close, overtaken in Atlantic crossings by the airlines with their speedy jet aircraft.

Myself, I obviously very much enjoy creating ocean liner books. But I also much enjoy sitting in a comfortable chair at home, say on a rainy Sunday afternoon, or in a quiet corner aboard a modern-day cruise ship, and reading a book about ships. Sometimes, I just look at the photos. This is just that kind of book – a grand and glorious review in pictures of some of the greatest ships to sail the seas. We have included text, of course, but it has not been our intention to provide every fact, detail, statistic about each ship. That's left to other books. But in a special way, this book adds, I feel, to our appreciation and understanding of the Great Atlantic Liners of the Twentieth Century.

Like those grand fleet reviews of bygone times, here is a modern-day review. So, sound the whistles – and turn the pages!

Bill Miller
Secaucus, New Jersey
Summer 2012

KAISER WILHELM DER GROSSE

By the last decade of the nineteenth century, the Germans – with growing technological and industrial might – were determined to surpass the dominant British and especially on the high seas. The North German Lloyd as well as the Hamburg-Amerika Line, rivals in their own right, were committed. Lloyd's effort came first when, in the fall of 1897, their 14,349 grt, 655-foot long *Kaiser Wilhelm der Grosse*, was commissioned. She captured the attention of the entire world, was dubbed 'the wonder ship' and ranked as the largest as well as the fastest ship afloat. She crossed from the Channel ports to New York in just short of six days. The Germans established a pattern aboard this 22-knot ship, the first of the so-called 'super liners', by grouping the funnels in two pairs. It made their ships instantly recognizable and had design elements as well – there was no need for four funnel shafts piercing through lower-deck public rooms.

OCEANIC

Above left: Launched in January 1899, the 17,300-ton *Oceanic* was the first vessel to exceed the *Great Eastern* in length, but not in tonnage. She ranked as the largest liner in the world, but not the fastest, averaging a less-than-record-breaking top speed of 19½ knots. Instead, the *Oceanic* was in the White Star Line mode of the day – 'slow and steady' service. For her seven-night crossings between Liverpool and New York, a first class suite cost £150 in 1900.

Above right: The 705-foot long *Oceanic* was a popular and largely successful ship, but had her share of mishaps. She was struck by lightning while in the River Mersey in 1900 and the main topmast was lost. In September 1901, she collided with and sank the small Irish steamer *Kincora* in fog off the Irish coast. Seven crew perished. In 1905, there was a crew mutiny aboard, protesting hard and severe working conditions. The mutiny was sparked by three dozen stokers.

Left: The *Oceanic* was commissioned as an armed merchant cruiser in August 1914, just as World War One began. But her days were numbered. Due to a navigational error, she was wrecked within a month, on September 8. She was stranded and then abandoned 20 miles west of the Shetland Islands. Partial scrapping began ten years later, in March 1924, and the hull was cut down to the waterline. Nearly 50 years later, in 1973, further salvage commenced and all remains were removed by 1979, seventy years since the *Oceanic* was launched.

Right: The *Oceanic* was to have had a sister ship, the *Olympic*, but the project was shelved and then canceled altogether following the death of Thomas Ismay, the White Star Line chairman, on November 23 1899. The order for the *Olympic* was replaced by one for 'the largest ships in the world' – the foursome that would become known as 'the Big Four'.

DEUTSCHLAND

Seen at her berth at Hoboken, New Jersey, in New York harbor, the 16,500 grt *Deutschland* was added in 1900 by the Hamburg-Amerika Line. She was an instant Blue Riband holder and held the trophy for trans-Atlantic speed for 6 years, but at great cost – the 684-foot long liner was plagued with excessive rattling and vibration. Thereafter, Hamburg-Amerika avoided chasing speed records, but placed its emphasis instead on size, luxury and comfort.

The 2,050-passenger *Deutschland*, seen here outbound off Lower Manhattan, was converted in 1911 to the all-white, all-first class cruise ship *Victoria Luise*. She survived World War One, was allowed to remain with the Germans and then sailed until 1925, but as the demoded, twin-funneled migrant ship *Hansa*.

CELTIC

Left: Record-breaker! When the 21,000-ton *Celtic* reached New York from Liverpool for the first time in August 1901, the outer reaches of the harbor had to be specially dredged and deepened. Using the very traditional four-mast design (which reminded the public of the great nineteenth-century sailing ships), she introduced a new trend: great size and great comfort, but coupled with only moderate speed. She made only 16 knots and therefore could operate on a more cost-efficient 280 tons of coal per day. The 700-foot long *Celtic* was a traditional three-class liner – 347 in first class, 160 in second class and 2,350 in third class.

Right: Early cruising! In February 1902, in a very early version of cruising, the *Celtic* departed from New York on a 35-day cruise around the Mediterranean. It was immensely popular – 800 passengers were booked for the entire voyage, which included Egypt and the Holy Land. In the end, the *Celtic* was wrecked near Cobh in December 1928 and her remains demolished in 1933.

KRONPRINZ WILHELM

Shown off Cherbourg, the 14,908 grt *Kronprinz Wilhelm* was the second of the big North German Lloyd liners – the *Kaiser Wilhelm der Grosse* (1897), *Kronprinz Wilhelm* (1901), *Kaiser Wilhelm II* (1903) and finally the *Kronprinzessin Cecilie* (1906). Noted for their very fine first class luxuries, a top-deck cabin could cost $2,000 for a seven-night crossing.

CEDRIC

Completed in 1903, the accommodations aboard White Star's *Cedric* were advertised as being 'an improvement' over her otherwise twin sister, the *Celtic*.

Cedric at New York's Pier 59. In April 1912, the *Cedric* was here after the *Titanic* sank. She was ordered to delay her sailing and remain in port until the rescue ship, Cunard's *Carpathia*, arrived with the 705 survivors. Those who wished could return to England and Ireland onboard the *Cedric*. This included the crew members who were not needed for the Court of Inquiry hearings. When she was sold for scrap in 1932, in the height of the Depression, the 21,000-ton liner realized only $75,000.

BALTIC

Above: During construction at Belfast in 1903, 20 feet was added to the midships of the *Baltic* in order that she would be the world's largest liner. This also added over 2,800 gross tons and made her a full 726 feet in length.

*Above right:*The 23,876-ton *Baltic* rescued 1,260 survivors from the collision between the *Republic*, also a White Star liner, and the Italian *Florida*, on January 23 1909. Three years later, on the afternoon of April 14 1912, the *Baltic* sent a message warning that she was slowing down, almost to a crawl, because of ice. The message was sent to her fleetmate, the brand new *Titanic*, which rammed an iceberg that same night.

Right: In May 1917, just after the US entered World War One, the *Baltic* carried the very first American troops to Europe. A commemorative plaque remained aboard until the ship was scrapped in far-off Osaka, Japan in 1933.

KAISER WILHELM II

Seen departing from the Second Street pier in Hoboken, the 707-feet long *Kaiser Wilhelm II* was, like the other North German Lloyd four-stackers, a great public relations success. During her maiden visit to the Lloyd terminal in Hoboken, some 40,000 visitors looked over what was then the largest as well as the fastest liner afloat. This was greater than the entire population of the New Jersey town. The *Kaiser Wilhelm II* had especially sumptuous first class quarters, which dazzled the public. She was dubbed 'a castle of the sea'. Overall, she could carry 1,888 passengers, with her quarters being divided into 775 first class, 343 second class and 770 steerage.

Left: Curiously, three of the four Lloyd four-stackers fell into American hands during World War One. While the *Kaiser Wilhelm der Grosse* was sunk in August 1914, the *Kaiser Wilhelm II* became the troopship USS *Agamemnon*, the *Kronprinz Wilhelm* changed to USS *Von Steuben* while the last of the quartet, the *Kronprinzessin Cecilie*, was renamed USS *Mount Vernon*.

Opposite: The *Lusitania* and *Mauretania* were two of Cunard's best known liners – the *Lusitania* because of her tragic sinking in World War One, the *Mauretania* due to her long, successful, triumphant career. Using different shipbuilders, the 31,550 grt *Lusitania* came from Scotland, from the John Brown & Company shipyard on the Clyde. She was launched in July 1906 and quickly dubbed 'the Lucy'. At 787 feet in length, the Mersey Docks & Harbour Board had to specially dredge in and around the Landing Stage to accommodate the enormous *Lusitania* and her sister. Even new, larger harbor tenders were needed. Designed under Admiralty supervision, it was intended that such a large, fast liner could also be used as an armed merchant cruiser in case of war.

LUSITANIA

On the outside, the *Lusitania* differed from the *Mauretania* in being less cluttered along her upper decks. Having fewer ventilators and other obstructions, the four funnels aboard the *Lusitania* looked taller.

Opposite: On her second crossing to New York, the *Lusitania* took the Blue Riband from Germany's *Kaiser Wilhelm II* with an average speed just short of 24 knots.

Between voyages at Liverpool, neither *Lusitania* nor *Mauretania* actually docked, but were anchored at the Sloyne. Both were serviced by large tenders. The two Cunarders did come alongside the Princes Landing Stage to disembark and embark passengers. In this dramatic view, however, the *Lusitania* is arriving at specially-built Pier 56 at the foot of New York's West 14th Street. The year is 1909. The 800 feet long pier was used by Cunard until 1950, then by freighter companies and was finally demolished in 1993.

In this view, from 1907, construction of the Chelsea Piers at New York has not yet begun. The area would be developed with a stretch of ten piers in all, servicing the likes of the French Line, White Star Line, Red Star Line and Atlantic Transport Line. In the 1920s and 30s, the likes of the United States Lines, Anchor Line, Grace Line, Italian Line, Panama Pacific Line and Canadian Pacific would become tenants as well.

After World War One erupted in August 1914 and almost all ships were called up for military service, it was decided that it would be the *Lusitania* that would continue a monthly Liverpool–New York commercial service.

Seen here on a winter's day at Pier 56 in New York, the *Lusitania* was a tragic loss during the War and became immortal. In May 1915, en route from New York to Liverpool, she was torpedoed by a German U-boat off the southeastern coast of Ireland. Of the 1,959 passengers and crew onboard, 1,198 perished, including 128 neutral US citizens. It was the worst ocean liner tragedy of World War One and the first of several actions by the Germans that eventually brought the United States into the conflict.

MAURETANIA

Built on the Tyne at Newcastle, the *Mauretania* was a success from day one. On her sea trials, she reached a top speed of 27 knots and, following her maiden voyage in November 1907, she captured the Blue Riband, which she held for an extraordinary 22 years.

The accommodations aboard the 31,938 grt *Mauretania* were arranged for 560 in first class, 475 second class and 1,300 third class.

Above: Like all ships, the *Mauretania* suffered the occasional mishap. In January 1908, her forward derricks were uplifted during a fierce Atlantic gale and smashed into the bridge windows.

Left: The 790 feet long *Mauretania* looked different from her near-sister, the *Lusitania.* The *Mauretania* was more cluttered on her upper decks, had more ventilators and had thicker steam pipes attached to her funnels.

Above: Between 1907 and 1914, the *Mauretania* – known affectionately as the 'Maury' – established herself as one of the most popular and profitable big liners on the Atlantic.

Left: The North Atlantic liner business was fiercely competitive. Cunard was included. In December 1910, the *Mauretania* offered – as the fastest ship afloat – a special twelve-day round trip between Liverpool and New York and then return to Liverpool. The attempt failed, however, when the Cunard flagship reached Liverpool instead on the thirteenth day.

Above left: In July 1910, the *Mauretania* was present for the grand opening of the Gladstone Graving Dock at Liverpool and was later inspected by King George V and Queen Mary.

Above right: During World War One, the *Mauretania* served mostly as a troopship, but in 1915–16 was used as a white-hulled hospital ship.

In 1932, in the twilight of her career and with the Depression deepening, the *Mauretania* was painted all-white and used for cruising. She even offered overnight 'booze cruises' from New York for $10 per person. She was now fondly known as the 'Grand Old Lady'.

Right: On September 26 1934, the day the *Queen Mary* was launched on the Clyde, the 27-year-old *Mauretania* departed from New York for the last time. Afterward, she was laid-up at Southampton pending disposal.

Far right: On July 1 1935, the *Mauretania* left Southampton for Rosyth and the breakers. Just before, some of her interior fittings were auctioned off.

At Rosyth, the legendary *Mauretania* faces her final days. Soon she will be demolished, ending the career of one of the Atlantic's greatest liners.

ADRIATIC

Right: There has long been a theory that a fifth ship for White Star's 'Big Four' was planned, but that ideas changed and instead such a ship became the *Amerika* for the Hamburg-Amerika Line. Briefly the world's largest ship in 1906–07, the 24,541-ton *Adriatic* had the first indoor pool and Turkish bath aboard an Atlantic liner. Used on the Liverpool–New York service, the 2,825-passenger *Adriatic* and her three sisters and near-sisters were very popular. On May 5 1912, Bruce Ismay, the White Star chairman who survived the sinking of the *Titanic*, returned to England aboard the *Adriatic*.

Left: In April 1919, following war service, the *Adriatic* brought five members of the Dixieland Jazz Band to Liverpool. It was the first time jazz had come to Britain.

GEORGE WASHINGTON

Left: With her four masts and pencil-thin twin stacks, this ship was a close cousin to White Star's 'Big Four' – *Celtic, Cedric, Baltic* and *Adriatic.* Dubbed 'the Big George', she was the world's largest liner for a short time. Deeply interested in the booming, very busy and highly profitable westbound immigrant trade (for the Germans as well as other Europeans), both the North German Lloyd and the Hamburg-Amerika Line began using American names as a way of luring more migrants on their ships. It was widely believed, although erroneously, that immigrants gained easier entry into the United States through Ellis Island if they were arriving aboard a ship with an American name.

Right: A view of the stern of *George Washington*, taken while she was in dry dock.

OLYMPIC

An important and a large ship, she has perhaps gained most fame and attention for being a sister ship to the immortal *Titanic*. The *Olympic* was the first sister, the first White Star liner with four funnels and the biggest ship afloat in 1911. But unlike the *Titanic* and their similar fleetmate *Britannic*, the *Olympic* had a long and largely successful career.

Shown here in the Thompson Graving Dock at the Harland & Wolff shipyard at Belfast, the 882-foot long *Olympic* was to be White Star's largest and finest ship, and the public was already fascinated. The original design had been for three funnels, but was changed with the added fourth 'dummy' stack (which was sometimes used as a galley exhaust).

At Southampton prior to her maiden voyage to Cherbourg, Queenstown and then onward to New York in June 1911.

The second class section of the *Olympic*'s Boat Deck.

On her maiden crossing, it took the 45,324 grt *Olympic* 5 days, 16 hours to reach New York.

The Chelsea Piers along New York's West Side were created especially for the likes of a new generation of larger, longer Atlantic liners. But even at that, extensions had to be added to several piers for liners over 800 feet in length. The *Olympic* is seen arriving at Pier 59.

Olympic in New York following her maiden voyage. *Lusitania* can be seen departing in the background.

Left: Among British liners in 1911, the *Olympic* was the top competitor to Cunard's *Lusitania* and *Mauretania*.

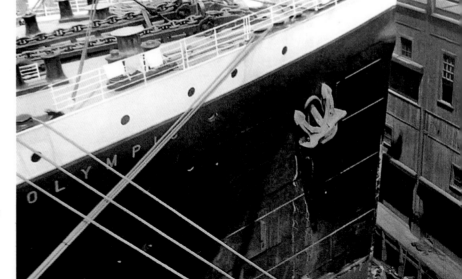

Right: In 1911, the *Olympic* was the largest ship to use the new Chelsea Piers, but it was a tight squeeze. Her bow is all but touching the dock head.

Above: On September 20 1911, in her maiden year, the *Olympic* was rammed in the Solent near Southampton by the British cruiser HMS *Hawke*. The *Olympic* was damaged aft on the starboard side, had afterward to travel to Belfast for repairs and altogether missed 6 weeks of sailings.

Right: After the sinking of the *Titanic* in April 1912, the *Olympic* was soon dispatched to Belfast for a thorough refit that refitted and upgraded her safety equipment. There were now forty-eight lifeboats in place, for example, instead of the original twenty. The refit cost $1.5 million.

Left: The *Olympic* was called to war duties in August 1914 and eventually (1915) repainted in camouflage, a scheme of disguising shapes also known as 'dazzle paint'.

Below left: Her heroics included an attempt to tow the mined battleship HMS *Audacious* in Loch Foyle in Ireland, on October 27 1914. She rescued the crew, but the stricken battleship later sank.

Below: Apart from later duties transporting soldiers on the North Atlantic, the *Olympic* spent considerable time in the Mediterranean. She had very close calls – twice she missed German torpedoes.

Left: Another heroic notation: in May 1918, the *Olympic* rammed and sank a German U-boat.

Right: Because of her great effort and heroics during the War, the *Olympic* was dubbed 'Old Reliable'. She was refitted and restored in 1919–20 and then resumed Atlantic commercial service. In the process, she was converted from coal to oil fuel, which reduced her engine room staff from 246 to 60.

Once back in service and highly popular, the *Olympic* had the occasional mishap. In March 1924, as an example, she collided at New York with the *Fort St George* of the Furness-Bermuda Line.

Above: Like most liners, the *Olympic* began to lose passengers and therefore any profit soon after the Wall Street Crash of October 1929. In the early 1930s, she was often detoured to inexpensive short cruises to earn at least some income. She is seen here in the floating dock at Southampton.

Right: A post-war view of the *Olympic*'s bow with evident dazzle paint coloring.

Above: In her final days, on May 10 1934, the *Olympic* rammed and sank the Nantucket Lightship in heavy fog. Eight were killed and her owners had to pay $500,000 in compensation.

Right: With a continuing downturn in Atlantic travel, the *Olympic* was retired in the spring of 1935, laid up at Southampton and later in the year sold to scrap metal merchants.

FRANCE

At 23,666 gross tons and 713 feet in length, the *France* was the first French super liner and their first and only four-stacker. Intended to be named *Picardie* and then *La Picardie*, she was launched in September 1910 and then completed in April 1912. At the time, there were four French ships also named *France* while a fifth was British. The *France* is seen here in Boston on a rare visit.

The *France* is preparing for another crossing as she loads at Le Havre.

Above left: While under construction in 1910–11, there was a bunker fire onboard and this delayed the *France*'s completion. Her maiden crossing from Le Havre to New York came within two weeks following the sinking of the *Titanic*.

Above right: In the 1920s, the *France* was teamed with the larger, newer *Paris* and then, in 1927, with the innovative *Ile de France*.

TITANIC

The sinking of the *Titanic* on April 14–15 1912 has made the ship immortal. She and the disaster have been the subjects of hundreds of books, magazine articles, TV documentaries, a Broadway musical and James Cameron's billion-dollar blockbuster film of 1997. The 46,320grt ship might just have been the second sister to the *Olympic*, but an unsinkable ship that actually sinks on no less than her maiden voyage creates a fascinating story. The ship is seen here just before launching at Belfast on May 31 1911.

This page: The *Titanic* is ready for a noontime launching while the *Olympic* will be departing from Belfast at 4:30 pm.

Opposite: The hull of the 882-foot long ship just begins to move from the launching slip.

Engineering genius. Although this image shows the three giant screws aboard *Olympic,* the same arrangement was used for. the *Titanic.*

Above: Fitting out with three funnels in place.

Right: Another view of the fitting-out. Slightly larger than the *Olympic,* the *Titanic* would be the largest ship in the world.

Some 3,000 workers were employed on the *Titanic* project at Harland & Wolff Ltd.

The liner being painted and readied for her trials.

Left: Another shipyard view.

Right: The *Titanic* is on the right, the *Olympic* on the left. The *Olympic* had returned to Belfast in February 1912 for adjustment and the fitting of a new propeller.

The Boat Deck of the *Titanic* as photographed at Southampton on April 12 1912.

Above: Another Boat Deck view.

Right: The giant liner at Southampton.

Above: A fine stern view of the ship in Belfast Lough, departing for sea trials.

Right: The *Titanic* dressed in flags for Good Friday, April 5 1912.

Above: Departure from Southampton at noon on April 10.

Right: Another departure view.

Right: On her departure from Southampton, the mammoth *Titanic* was attended by no less than eight tugs.

Below: An imposing sight: the *Titanic* in Southampton Water.

Left: Another view in Southampton Water.

Above: At Queenstown, the *Titanic*'s last port of call. When she departed, it is estimated that 1,320 passengers were aboard, along with 892 crew (the actual numbers have always varied).

Left: As is well known, the *Titanic* never completed her maiden voyage to New York. The tragedy has been exhaustively documented and analyzed. Suffice herein to say that the *Titanic* set off from Southampton on April 10 1912. She nearly collided with another liner (the *New York*), but four days later, just before midnight and in cold North Atlantic waters some 380 miles east of Newfoundland, the great liner had a far more serious collision. She sideswiped an iceberg that ripped a 300 feet long gash along her starboard side. The glitter and glory of her maiden crossing abruptly turned to horrific tragedy. Within 2½ hours, she sank in 12,000 feet of ocean water. Dramatically, the 'unsinkable' marvel lifted from the sea by the stern, broke in half and plunged to the bottom. Because there were too few lifeboats, an estimated 1,522 perished. The 705 survivors represented a scant 32 per cent of all those onboard.

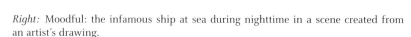

Right: Moodful: the infamous ship at sea during nighttime in a scene created from an artist's drawing.

IMPERATOR/BERENGARIA

Left: The *Imperator* was a ship of immense, almost extraordinary proportions for her time – 52,117 tons, 919 feet in length and able to carry 4,594 passengers in four classes. Ordered in 1910 and completed three years later, she was actually the first of three successively larger behemoths. The 54,000 grt, 950-foot long *Vaterland* followed in 1914 and the 56,000 grt, 956-foot long *Bismarck* was scheduled for 1915 (but never completed for the Germans owing to World War One). Hamburg-Amerika Line wanted every distinction other than record speed. At first, they seemed to succeed. The general public marveled at the mighty *Imperator*.

Below: To ensure that the *Imperator* surpassed the length of Cunard's forthcoming 901-foot long *Aquitania*, the *Imperator* was fitted with an ornamental, but otherwise useless eagle and globe mounted to the bow. This gave the German super ship added length. But it was soon ripped off during a furious Atlantic storm and was never replaced.

The *Imperator* had some serious blemishes. She was soon found to be top-heavy and easily rolled even in the calmest seas. Consequently, her towering funnels were cut down by 9 feet, interior decorations were refitted with lighter materials and tons of cement was poured along her bottom. But in the end, she was never fully free of her fragility.

Above: Seen here in the Hudson River, the *Berengaria* became one of the most popular Atlantic liners of the 1920s. She was paired on Cunard's express service with the *Aquitania* and *Mauretania.*

Left: After post-war allocation to the United States, the *Imperator* served briefly as the USS *Imperator* before being allocated to the British as reparations. She was then managed by Cunard and, beginning in February 1920, began making Liverpool–New York crossings for Cunard as the *Imperator.* Months later, in May, the *Imperator* and the incomplete *Bismarck* (which became the *Majestic* in 1922) were purchased jointly by Cunard and by White Star. A month later, the *Imperator* was switched to Southampton–New York service and, in April 1921, was renamed *Berengaria.*

Above: *Berengaria* is seen here with *Olympic* in Southampton.

Right: In this view, the *Berengaria* steams past battleships assembled for King George V's Silver Jubilee Fleet Review off Spithead in June 1935. The 52,226 grt *Berengaria* was facing hard times because of the Depression. Dubbed 'the Bargain-area' by loyalists, the ship offered more and more cheap cruises to fill her cabins. She was finally retired in March 1938 and later sold to scrappers, but was not entirely demolished until after World War Two, in 1946.

VATERLAND/LEVIATHAN

Above: Unfortunately, the giant *Vaterland* was at her New York berth, at the Second Street pier in Hoboken, when Germany went to war. The ship sat idle for almost three years until seized, in April 1917, once America entered the hostilities. She is seen here flying the Stars and Stripes at her Hoboken slip. Soon reactivated and becoming the USS *Leviathan*, she ranked as the largest troopship in that First War.

Left: In the years just prior to the dramatically untimely outbreak of World War One in August 1914, the managers of the Hamburg-Amerika Line could barely contain their excitement. They were building the three largest liners yet and the second, the 54,282 grt, 3,909-passenger *Vaterland*, was due in service in the spring of 1914. She is shown here in dry dock at Hamburg. Her details were all but mind-boggling: 1.5 million rivets, onboard bunkers for 9,000 tons of coal, space for 12,000 tons of cargo and a crew of 1,180. She carried a commodore, four deputy captains, seven nautical officers and twenty-nine engineers.

After the war, in 1921–23, the *Leviathan* underwent a two-year refit and restoration. Used on the New York–Cherbourg–Southampton run, her quarters were restyled for 3,391 passengers – 970 in first class, 542 in second class, 944 in third class and 935 in fourth class.

Above left: Shown in the big graving dock at the Boston Naval Shipyard, the 54,282 grt *Leviathan* was the flagship, despite her German heritage, of the entire US merchant marine. She lacked adequate running-mates on her express service sailings, unlike Cunard and White Star, each of which had three large liners that offered weekly sailings in each direction. The *Leviathan*'s popularity was further hindered by the general feeling that British and European liners offered better service. The *Leviathan* operated at a continuing loss.

Above right: American Prohibition laws further detracted from the *Leviathan*. She was a 'dry' ship.

Left: *Leviathan* at Southampton.

Right: The *Leviathan* lost more and more money by 1930, and then still more as the Depression set in. She was laid-up in 1932 then reactivated in 1934, but only for four voyages. Laid up thereafter at Hoboken, she returned to sea once more and departed for Scotland in January 1938 for scrapping.

AQUITANIA

Built by John Brown on the Clyde (who had to lengthen their building slip for her 901-foot long hull), the *Aquitania* was designed as the third, larger teammate of the highly successful *Lusitania* and *Mauretania*. She did not get a construction subsidy from the British government, however, and therefore had far fewer war components but instead 50 per cent more passenger capacity.

The 3,230-passenger *Aquitania* barely entered service in the spring of 1914 when World War One erupted. Used as an armed merchant cruiser and a hospital ship, but mostly as a troopship, she established a heroic record. Alone, she carried 30,000 troops to the Dardanelles, 25,000 patients from the Turkish war zone and then ferried 60,000 American troops across the Atlantic.

Right: Having served in two world wars, the *Aquitania* finished her Cunard duties in 1948–49 by running a Southampton–Halifax austerity service. She was finally decommissioned in November 1949 and, months later, was sold to scrappers in Scotland. With a crew of 250 onboard, she is seen here arriving at Faslane for the 'final rites'. The 36-year-old liner was the last four-stacker and established records that included steaming 3,000,000 miles and carrying 1,200,000 passengers.

Opposite: The 45,647 grt *Aquitania* was hugely popular and known as 'the Ship Beautiful' for her perfect proportions as well as her interior splendor. She had a long, colorful history and many notations. In May 1921, she crossed to New York with 2,750 passengers onboard but her stewards and waiters were on strike; not missing the sailing, the ship was staffed by Cunard office workers as well as volunteers.

BRITANNIC

The third of White Star Line's trio of luxurious express liners, seen here on the srocks, was to be called *Gigantic*, but in the wake of the *Titanic* disaster, she was given a less pretentious name.

The 903-foot long ship was launched at Belfast on February 26 1914 as the *Britannic*.

Intended for commercial sailings in 1915, the overall construction and completion of the 48,158 grt *Britannic* was delayed pending the outcome of the Court of Enquiry into the *Titanic* tragedy.

Intended for 2,573 passengers in three classes, the *Britannic* never entered White Star Line service. War started in August and so her completion was delayed and then reworked. She was finally finished in November 1915 as a hospital ship in International Red Cross livery. She is seen here at Belfast with dummy battleships (designed to fool the enemy as to location of the British fleet) alongside and the *Olympic* behind.

Shown at Southampton in 1916, the *Britannic* as a hospital ship had a capacity of over 3,300 beds. This was the second highest at the time, surpassed only by the *Aquitania* with 4,182 beds.

As originally designed by the White Star Line, the *Britannic* had rather unique if ungainly lattice gantry davits which could launch four lifeboats at one time.

Britannic at Mudros. This town on the island of Lemnos was an important Allied base during the Gallipoli campaign.

The *Britannic* would never make a transatlantic crossing, but was sent instead to the Mediterranean, sailing from Southampton to Alexandria as well as from Marseilles. She often bunkered at Naples.

On November 21 1916, when only a year old, the *Britannic* ran into a German laid mine in the Aegean, exploded and sank with the loss of twenty-one lives. She was the largest liner to be lost in World War One. Union-Castle Line's *Braemar Castle*, also a passenger ship, struck a mine in the same area two days later and also sank.

The *Britannic* was one of the least known big liners of her time. But along with the sinking of the *Titanic* just four years before, her demise was to signal the slow, gradual decline of once prosperous and mighty White Star Line.

The passenger fittings for the *Britannic* were never used and remained in storage at Belfast. After the war, in the summer of 1919, they were auctioned off, sold but often for comparatively low, post-war prices.

The disintegrated wreckage in the Aegean Sea of the *Britannic* was discovered by Jacques Cousteau's dive vessel *Calypso* in 1976.

MAJESTIC

Above left: Seen here in the King George V Graving Dock at Southampton, the 56,551 grt *Majestic* was intended to be the *Bismarck*, the third of the German giants built between 1912 and 1915. She never set sail and, after the war ended, she was allocated as reparations to the British and, in 1922, began sailing as the *Majestic*, the flagship of the White Star Line. She was compensation for the loss of the *Britannic*. The 956-foot long *Majestic* was also listed as the world's largest liner, a record held until surpassed by the *Normandie* in 1935.

Above right: The 2,145-passenger *Majestic* was immediately popular. She was inspected by King George V and Queen Mary during Cowes Week in August 1922, was said to be the second fastest liner on the Atlantic and often carried record numbers of passengers. She was fondly dubbed the 'Magic Stick' and is seen in this view when sailing from New York's Pier 61.

Left: The *Majestic* was teamed with the *Olympic* and *Homeric* as part of White Star Line's three-ship express service between Southampton, Cherbourg and New York.

Right: Shown here in the big floating dry dock at Southampton, a crack developed along the side of the *Majestic*'s hull in 1924. Her plating was strengthened, but her general strength was thereafter always suspected by White Star engineers.

In her final years and as the Atlantic liner trade slumped because of the Depression, in the 1930s the *Majestic* was often sent on short, inexpensive cruises from New York including cheap, overnight 'booze cruises'. But months before Cunard-White Star's *Queen Mary* was commissioned, the *Majestic* was retired. Sold to scrappers, she was then resold to the British Admiralty for use as HMS *Caledonia*, a moored naval cadets' training ship. She was swept by fire in September 1939, however, and then sank. Later salvaged, she was gradually scrapped over the next three years.

PARIS

Above: Seen departing from New York's Pier 57, the 34,569 grt *Paris* was intended to enter French Line transatlantic service in 1916. But owing to World War One, she was only launched in September 1916 and then promptly laid up. Construction resumed three years later, in 1919, and the 764-feet long liner was completed in the spring of 1921.

Left: Like many liners, the *Paris* had her share of mishaps. As an example, in April 1928, with 300 passengers onboard, she ran aground off Brooklyn, in New York harbor.

Above left: Seen berthed at Pier 88 in New York, the *Paris* was intended in 1937–38 to become a white-hulled, full-time cruise ship, but the idea never came to pass. She was fated, however, to succumb to a problem common to French passenger ships: fire. She burned out and then capsized at Le Havre in April 1939. Her wreckage was not removed, however, until after World War Two ended, in 1947.

ILE DE FRANCE

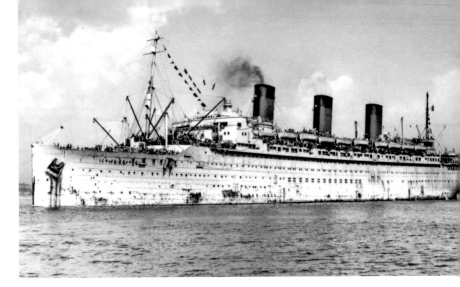

When the 43,153 grt *Ile de France* was completed in the spring of 1927, she ranked as the sixth largest liner afloat. She was the flagship of the French merchant marine, said to be the best fed liner on the Atlantic, carried more first class passengers than any other liner and introduced a new style of interior decor called moderne (and later dubbed Art Deco). She was one of the most important ships of the twentieth century – and one of the most popular and beloved. She is seen here, however, still in gray wartime coloring in a postwar view, in 1946.

After strenuous wartime trooping (up to 9,000 soldier-passengers per voyage), the 791-foot long *Ile de France* ran an austerity liner service between Cherbourg and New York in 1946–47. Afterward, she underwent a two-year refit that included replacing her original three funnels with two new stacks. In this view, she is being docked unassisted during a New York harbor tugboat strike on February 15 1957. Some 4,000 tug and barge crews refused to work.

Above left: Late in her life, the *Ile* became a heroic ship. She rescued 753 passengers and crew on July 26 1956 from the sinking Italian liner *Andrea Doria*. Bound for Europe, the *Ile* stood by, then reversed course and returned to Pier 88.

Above right: After being retired from French Line service in November 1958, the Sheraton Corporation considered buying the 31-year-old liner and making her over as a floating hotel on Martinique in the French West Indies. A sale never materialized; the ship was finally sold to Japanese scrappers.

EUROPA

As the idea of simultaneous maiden voyages faded, the *Europa* was to be the first to be commissioned. However, on March 29 1929, while fitting out, she was swept by fire and nearly destroyed. The damages were so severe it was thought that the brand new, 936-foot long liner might have to be scrapped. She was repaired, but delivered one year late. As with her near-sister, the original flat funnels aboard the *Europa* had to be raised in height because of far too much smoke and soot falling on the aft passenger decks.

Above left: It was a publicity department's dream come true. There had been a plan in 1928 to have the brand new German super liners *Europa* and *Bremen* cross together from Bremerhaven to New York and simultaneously break the Atlantic speed record. The record was then held by Britain's *Mauretania*. Intended to be 35,000 tonners, the designs for the two German liners were actually changed during the early stages of construction to 50,000 tons, and with more powerful engines. It was intended that the *Europa* and *Bremen* would be the premier liners of the world. The *Europa* was launched first, at Hamburg on August 15 1928; the *Bremen* followed a day later, but at Bremen.

Above right: *Europa* fitting out in Hamburg in 1930.

Left: New York was crammed with ships in the 1930s, such that North German Lloyd could not lease adequate pier space for the giant *Europa* and *Bremen*. And so they had to use 1,700 feet long Pier 4 of the Brooklyn Army Terminal, located in the port's Lower Bay. The 2,024-passenger *Europa* is shown here berthed in Brooklyn. Lloyd was able to relocate, in 1934, to the more convenient Pier 86 at the foot of West 46th Street in Manhattan.

Above: The *Europa* sat out the war unused and neglected, but then was seized by American invasion forces (in May 1945) before being given to the French as reparations. She re-emerged as the greatly refitted *Liberte* in the summer of 1950 and so began a second career.

BREMEN

Above left: The *Europa* and *Bremen* differed in ways (including the shapes of their funnels), but were close sisters and together with a third ship, the smaller *Columbus*, maintained a weekly service to and from New York. Because of a fire and a year's delay with the *Europa*, the 51,656 grt *Bremen* became the first of the new pair to enter service. On her maiden voyage, in July 1929, she took the Blue Riband from Cunard's *Mauretania*.

Above right: Shown here in New York's Lower Bay and with her taller funnels, the *Bremen* returned to Germany in the fall of 1939 as World War Two began. She never sailed again. She was destroyed by fire at her berth in March 1941, much of her remains scrapped and the final pieces deliberately sunk in the Weser River.

Below left: Seen here at Bremerhaven, the *Bremen* and her sister were Germany's largest, finest and most prestigious ships. Eventually, they would fly the Nazi flag but subsequently carried fewer passengers.

EMPRESS OF BRITAIN

Left: Canadian Pacific, the great transportation combine, had liner services across the Atlantic as well as the Pacific. To enhance their Atlantic run to eastern Canada, the company added its largest and grandest liner, the 42,348 grt *Empress of Britain*, in 1931. Built on the Clyde in Scotland (as shown), she was one of the great liners of the 1930s.

Right: Cleverly balanced, the 758-foot long *Empress* – with her trio of buff-colored, oversized funnels – was designed to spend about eight months in trans-ocean service and then another three to four months on long, luxurious world cruises from New York.

Seen entering the King George V Graving Dock at Southampton with the *Olympic* behind, the *Empress of Britain* was called to war, but quickly became a casualty, being damaged by Nazi bombers and then sunk by an enemy U-Boat off Ireland in October 1940.

NORMANDIE

Above left: The 82,799-grt *Normandie* was, in many ways, the most sensational, luxurious and legendary super liner of the twentieth century. Everything about her – from her exterior design to her Art Deco interiors to her superb kitchens – was newsworthy. When she was launched at St Nazaire, there were 200,000 spectators present. Her godmother was Madame Lebrun, the First Lady of France. Numerous names had been considered for the 1,028 feet long ship, the pride of the French fleet, including *General Pershing*, *Napoleon* and *Jeanne d'Arc*. *La Belle France* was reportedly a strong contender. When *Normandie* was selected, the French Academy insisted that it should be *La Normandie*. The French Line itself settled on *Normandie*.

Above right: Similar to Britain's *Queen Mary*, which was building at the same time, the *Normandie*'s construction was halted for a time (two years in all) and she was not delivered until the spring of 1935. She did her final trials off the Brittany coast and reached full speed but with the absence of a bow wave and wake.

Above: Normandie was launched on October 29 1932, three years to the day after the Wall Street Crash.

Left: When the 1,972-passenger *Normandie* first arrived in New York on June 3 1935, she was the largest liner afloat, stunning inside and out, and captured the prized Blue Riband with an average speed of 29.94 knots. Upon arrival, she flew a 30 feet long pennant (one foot for each knot). Ten tugs berthed the flag-bedecked liner at the 1,100 feet long Pier 88, which was built especially for her.

Right: During the ship's first winter overhaul, in 1935–36, the hull was strengthened, the three-bladed propellers replaced by a four-bladed type and an otherwise unnecessary deckhouse was added to push the ship's tonnage up from 79,280 grt to 82,799 grt so as to surpass the tonnage of 81,235 for Cunard's *Queen Mary*, which was due out in May 1936.

Far right: At Le Havre in the spring of 1936, preparing to sail for New York, one of the *Normandie*'s propellers dropped off. The liner was hurriedly dry docked and synchronized for three screws instead of four. Sailing only hours late, the *Normandie* suffered, however, from unusual vibration during that roundtrip voyage.

Left: The *Normandie* and *Queen Mary* fiercely competed for the Blue Riband, beginning in 1936, but by August 1938 it went firmly to the Cunarder. Famous, celebrated and a public relations 'dreamboat', the *Normandie* was not a great commercial success, unfortunately. In 139 crossings between 1935 and 1939, she averaged only 59 per cent of capacity.

Right: As war clouds were mounting in Europe, the *Normandie* was laid up at Pier 88 in late August 1939. She was soon joined by the *Queen Mary*, repainted in gray at the adjacent Pier 90. While the Cunarder became a heroic, highly useful troopship, the French flagship would never sail again. While being converted for war use, she caught fire on February 9 1942, later capsized and her salvaged, reduced remains were scrapped in 1946–47.

REX

It is sadly ironic to note that the glorious *Rex* actually sailed for less than eight years. The onset of World War Two shortened her commercial days and her life span as well. When she was destroyed in an Allied attack in September 1944, she was all but twelve years old. Similarly, her Italian Line running-mate, the *Conte di Savoia*, saw less than eight years of active service as well; the *Bremen* had ten years; the *Empress of Britain* eight years; and, possibly saddest of all the Atlantic super liners of the 1930s, the brilliant *Normandie* sailed for little more than four years.

The *Rex* was also a speed champion – she held the Blue Riband from August 1933 until May 1935.

CONTE DI SAVOIA

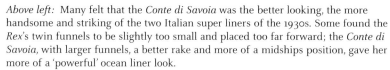

Above left: Many felt that the *Conte di Savoia* was the better looking, the more handsome and striking of the two Italian super liners of the 1930s. Some found the *Rex*'s twin funnels to be slightly too small and placed too far forward; the *Conte di Savoia*, with larger funnels, a better rake and more of a midships position, gave her more of a 'powerful' ocean liner look.

Above right: Seen at New York's Pier 92, the quarters onboard the 814-foot long *Conte di Savoia* were grouped as 500 in first class, 366 second class, 412 tourist class and 922 third class.

Below right: Burnt out during World War Two, on September 11 1943, her hull was thought to have potential for rebuilding in the late 1940s. There was a plan to rebuild the ship, but as a 2,500-capacity, all-third class immigrant ship. In the final appraisal, the idea never came to pass and so the remains of the *Conte di Savoia* were scrapped in 1950. Comparatively, the remains of the capsized *Rex* were broken up between 1947 and 1958.

QUEEN MARY

While progressive and enduring, the Cunard Line was actually a conservative firm. They rarely looked to stark innovation or modernism. Consequently, when the Liverpool-based firm planned their first super liner of the 1930s, they looked to the past in some ways and even reviewed the plans for the *Aquitania* of 1914. While using 1930s Art Deco as a basic style for her interior decor, her exterior was quite traditional, especially when compared to the more advanced, sleek *Normandie*. As King George V said, the 81,235 grt *Queen Mary* was a 'stately ship'. She was, of course, a huge success and sailed for 31 years.

As built, the *Queen Mary* carried a full crew of 1,285. To be teamed with a second super liner, the two Cunarders were the very first pair of passenger ships to maintain a weekly express service on the Atlantic. As planned, the *Queen Mary* was designed to complete a crossing within a week and to do forty-four per year. This was based on 112 hours from Cherbourg to New York's Ambrose Light as well as 45–50 hours' turnaround at Southampton and 24–30 hours at New York. This represented a consistent speed of 29 knots in all weather conditions.

During the war, the *Queen Mary* and the *Queen Elizabeth* were the world's largest and most important troopships. On the Atlantic, beginning in January 1942, they averaged 15,000 soldiers per voyage. In July 1943, the *Queen Mary* established an all-time record: 16,683 onboard for one voyage. Not resuming commercial service until July 1947, the *Queen Mary* even served in the immediate post-war years by carrying returning troops, displaced persons, medical patients and war brides.

The *Queen Mary* endured for 31 years, sailing for Cunard until the fall of 1967. She made 1,000 crossings, carried 2,100,000 passengers and steamed 3,700,000 miles. Ironically, she never visited her homeport of Liverpool. Facing the scrappers in the end, she was finally sold to the City of Long Beach in California, where she lives on to this day as a museum, hotel and collection of shops.

NIEUW AMSTERDAM

The *Nieuw Amsterdam* was Holland's most beloved liner, a symbol of post-war liberation and one of the most beautiful ocean liners ever to sail. Launched in April 1937, she was commissioned a year later for service between Rotterdam, Southampton, Boulogne and New York. The 36,287 grt *Nieuw Amsterdam* was an instant success.

After heroic, but almost exhausting, duties as a 9,000-capacity troopship during World War Two, the *Nieuw Amsterdam* made her first triumphant return to the port of Rotterdam in April 1946. A symbol of liberation, peace and renewal, the 758-feet long liner – still in wartime gray coloring – was affectionately dubbed 'the Darling of the Dutch'.

When the *Nieuw Amsterdam* was retired in December 1973, there was a rumor that the City of Rotterdam would buy the 36-year-old liner, perhaps for use as a museum and hotel. The idea never came to pass and instead she finished her long, distinguished career in a Taiwanese scrap yard.

MAURETANIA (II)

Right: After being commissioned in June 1939, the 'new' *Mauretania* was said to be able to substitute for one of the far larger and faster *Queens* on the Southampton–Cherbourg–New York express service. At 29 knots, the *Queens* could make the passage in five days; the *Mauretania*, at 23 knots, could do it in six days.

During her maiden crossing to New York in June 1939, there were ten passengers onboard who had been on the maiden voyage of the first *Mauretania*, 32 years earlier in 1907. This second *Mauretania* established herself, after World War Two, as a very popular Atlantic liner and as a winter cruise ship, sailing mostly from New York to the Caribbean on two-week itineraries.

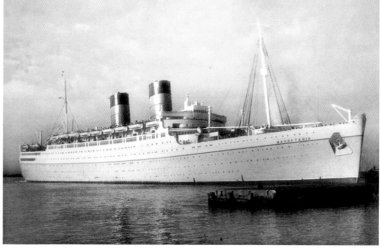

Like almost all Atlantic liners, the 35,655 grt *Mauretania* was struggling by the early 1960s. Airline competition had far overtaken ocean liners. In September 1962, the *Mauretania* was repainted in Cunard's 'cruising green' for increased cruise service as well as a highly unsuccessful stint in Mediterranean–New York liner service. The 772-foot long ship went prematurely to the breakers in November 1965.

AMERICA

Right: Intended for North Atlantic liner service beginning in the summer of 1940, the war in Europe altered plans and the 723-feet long liner was kept closer to home, for cruising and inter-coastal voyages between New York and California. She spent the war as the high-capacity troopship USS *West Point*.

Left: When the 33,900 grt *America* was ordered in 1936, she was the first of the US government's Merchant Marine Act plan to build 6,000 merchant ships. It would end with the completion of another liner, the *United States*, in 1952. The *America*, named by Mrs Franklin D. Roosevelt at its launching on August 31 1939, ranked as the largest liner yet built in an American shipyard.

Left: America in her war colors. As USS *West Point*, she served as a troop transport throughout the Second World War in both the Atlantic and the Pacific.

Right: A great prelude to the speedy, far larger *United States*, the *America* finally entered commercial service in November 1946. She was a very popular ship, said to be among the best in the US liner fleet, until phased out in 1964. Afterward, she became a Greek tourist and immigrant ship, the *Australis*.

QUEEN ELIZABETH

The twin-funnel *Queen Elizabeth* was considered one of the best looking liners of her time. She had perfect balance and proportion, and actually looked more contemporary than the earlier *Queen Mary*. The *Elizabeth* was larger, ranking as the largest liner ever built (a record unbeaten until 1996, by the 101,000 grt cruise ship *Carnival Destiny*), but officially not as fast as the record-breaking *Queen Mary* (which held the Blue Riband for sixteen years, from 1936 until 1952). The 83,673 grt, 1,031-foot long *Queen Elizabeth* was due to enter service in April 1940 and thereby complete Cunard's two-ship express service. But the outbreak of war changed those plans and instead she served as a gray-painted, 15,000-capacity troopship until 1946.

Right: By the early 1960s, however, the *Queen Elizabeth* (and the *Queen Mary*) began running occasional cruises to offset increasing losses on the Atlantic. In 1965, the *Queen Elizabeth* was given an extensive refit that included such cruising amenities as complete air-conditioning, more private bathrooms in cabins and an open-air swimming pool.

Opposite: The 2,233-passenger, three-class *Queen Elizabeth* finally entered commercial service in November 1946. The 1,957-berth *Queen Mary* joined her in the following July. By the mid-1950s, Cunard had fourteen liners on the Atlantic, serving New York as well as Quebec and Montreal, with the promotional slogan: 'Getting there is half the fun!' In the 1950s, both *Queens* were hugely successful and were often booked to capacity.

Retired by Cunard in the fall of 1968, the *Queen Elizabeth* went to Port Everglades in Florida, where she was to become an East Coast version (hotel, museum, shops) of the *Queen Mary* in southern California. But the project failed and the liner was later auctioned off (in 1970) and sold to a Chinese shipping tycoon who planned to reactivate the ship as the floating university-cruise ship *Seawise University*. But on the eve of her first departure, on January 9 1972, she caught fire in Hong Kong harbor, capsized and later her remains were scrapped.

CARONIA

In the 1950s especially, the all-green *Caronia* was often said to be the most luxurious liner not only in the then large Cunard fleet, but also in the world. Used for long, luxurious cruising, carrying a club-like 600 or so passengers being looked after by 600 mostly handpicked crew, she had a select, often very loyal following. Some passengers 'lived' onboard for months and even years at a time and while one lady established an all-time record: she remained aboard for fourteen years.

Left: The 34,183 grt *Caronia*'s green coloring was used as a heat-resistant in the tropics, but it also gave her an added, unique identity. She was quickly dubbed the 'Green Goddess'.

Right: Here, *Caronia* is seen in Wellington Harbor, New Zealand.

Mostly, the *Caronia* did one, two and three-month-long cruises. Without present-day easy air connections, passengers did the entire voyage. As a sample voyage, on January 21 1958, the *Caronia* set off from New York's Pier 90 for a 110-day cruise around the world. Ports of call read: Trinidad, Bahia, Rio de Janeiro, Tristan da Cunha, Cape Town, Durban, Zanzibar, Port Victoria, Bombay, Colombo, Singapore, Bangkok, Bali, Manila, Hong Kong, Yokohama, Honolulu, Long Beach, Acapulco, Balboa and Cristobal. Fares began at $3,200.

Caronia is seen here arriving at Long Beach, California, on an earlier voyage around the world, from 1955.

UNITED STATES

The 53,329 grt *United States* was possibly the most brilliant liner of the twentieth century. Designed during World War Two and built in the late 1940s, she came about due to the US government's concern about carrying large numbers of troops (15–18,000) on a high-speed vessel. Another world war was thought to be imminent by some officials. Indeed, the 990-foot long *United States* was a troopship disguised and completed as an ocean liner. She was best of American postwar design, construction and technology. She did an astounding 43 knots during her trials, went 20 knots in full reverse and had exceptional safety standards. On her maiden crossing from New York to Southampton in July 1952, she crossed in 3 days and 10 hours. Her average speed was 35.59 knots.

Using her 33-knot operating speed, the *United States* maintained a service of New York to Le Havre and Southampton in five days, and to Bremerhaven in six days. In 1959, minimum fares were $380 in first class, $260 in cabin class and $197 in tourist class. In her first decade, until the early 1960s, the 1,928-berth ship was a blazing success.

Left: Perhaps one of the best known stories about the great safety onboard the $75 million *United States* concerned the wood onboard. It was often said that there was absolutely no wood onboard, except in the butcher's block and the Steinway pianos.

Below: Heavily subsidized by the US government, the *United States* sailed for only 17 years, until laid up in November 1969. These days, she has been idle for 43 years, currently lying at Philadelphia. Preservation groups hope to restore her as a museum, hotel and entertainment center.

FRANCE (II)

The 66,348 grt *France* was the last of the big French liners. Built as a replacement for both the aged *Ile de France* and *Liberte*, she entered service in the winter of 1962. She was modern, elegant, very popular and expectedly well fed. Used mostly for crossings, she also did some cruising, including two voyages around the world (featuring calls at Sydney, as in this view). She survived for only twelve years, until retired by the French in 1974. She was revived, however, as the cruise ship *Norway*, sailing from 1980 until 2003 and then finally being scrapped in India in 2009.

ROTTERDAM

Left: As the glorious, 1938-built *Nieuw Amsterdam* aged in the 1950s, the Holland America Line needed a new flagship. This ship was completed in the summer of 1959 as the 1,456-passenger *Rotterdam.* Modern and contemporary, the 748-footer was notable in dispensing with the conventional funnel and instead having twin uptakes placed aft. She is seen here arriving at New York.

Above: The liner has endured – in 2010 she arrived in Rotterdam for use as a moored hotel, museum and entertainment center.

LEONARDO DA VINCI

One of the most handsome liners of her time, the 33,340 grt *Leonardo da Vinci* was built at Genoa, Italy, and completed in 1960 as a replacement for another Italian liner, the *Andrea Doria*, which sank off the American East Coast in July 1956. The *da Vinci* was larger, more modern and was considered the finest example in her day of Italian naval design, engineering and expectedly safety. Her engine room spaces were reportedly twice the size needed so that the 1,326-berth ship could be converted, perhaps by 1965, to nuclear power.

With six swimming pools, modern Italian decor and as many as 80 per cent of her tourist class cabins with private shower & toilet facilities, the 763-foot long *Leonardo da Vinci* was a great success in her early years. She sailed regularly between Naples, Genoa, Cannes, Gibraltar and New York.

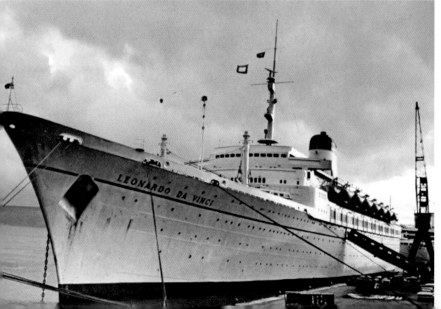

She was repainted in all-white in 1966 and thereafter spent more and more time in the expanding cruise business. Italian Line faded out of the passenger ship business in the 1970s and it was the *Leonardo da Vinci* that made the final crossing from New York in June 1976. Except for the *Queen Elizabeth 2* and Poland's little *Stefan Batory*, it was the end of the trans-Atlantic liner era. Later sent to lay up, the *da Vinci* caught fire in July 1980, burned out and was scrapped by 1982. By then, the greatest and grandest era of the Atlantic liners was long gone.

BIBLIOGRAPHY

Braynard, Frank O. *Lives of the Liners*. New York: Cornell Maritime Press, 1947.

Crowdy, Michael & O'Donoghue, Kevin (editors). *Marine News*. Kendal, Cumbria, England: World Ship Society 1963–2012.

Devol, George & Cassidy, Thomas (editors). *Ocean & Cruise News*. Stamford, Connecticut: World Ocean & Cruise Liner Society, 1980–2012.

Dunn, Laurence. *Passenger Liners*. Southampton, England: Adlard Coles Ltd, 1961.

— *Passenger Liners* (revised edition). Southampton, England: Adlard Coles Ltd, 1965.

Haws, Duncan. *Merchant Fleets: Cunard Line*. Hereford, England: TCL Publications, 1987.

Mayes, William. *Cruise Ships* (revised 3rd edition). Windsor, England: Overview Press Ltd, 2011.

Miller, William H. *British Ocean Liners: A Twilight Era 1960–85*. New York: W. W. Norton & Co, 1986.

— *Crossing the Atlantic*. Portland, Oregon: Graphic Arts Books, 2005.

— *The First Great Ocean Liners in Photographs: 1897–1927*. New York, New York: Dover Publications Inc, 1984.

— *German Ocean Liners of the 20th Century*. Wellingborough, Northamptonshire, England, 1989.

— *The Great Luxury Liners 1927–54*. New York: Dover Publications Inc, 1981.

— *Ocean Liner Chronicles*. London: Carmania Press Ltd, 2001.

— *Pictorial Encyclopedia of Ocean Liners, 1864–1994*. Mineola, New York: Dover Publications Inc, 1995.

— *Picture History of American Passenger Ships.* Mineola, New York: Dover Publications Inc, 2001.

— *Picture History of British Ocean Liners.* Mineola, New York: Dover Publications Inc, 2001.

— *Picture History of the Cunard Line 1840–1990.* New York: Dover Publications Inc, 1991.

— *Picture History of German & Dutch Passenger Ships.* New York: Dover Publications Inc, 2002.

— *Picture History of the Italian Line 1932–1977.* New York: Dover Publications Inc, 1999.

— *The QE2: A Picture History.* New York: Dover Publications Inc, 2008.

Steamboat Bill. East Providence, Rhode Island: Steamship Historical Society of America Inc, 1963–2012.

Ships Monthly. Burton-on-Trent, Staffordshire, England, 1980–2012.